THE
FINAL
SCORE

THE FINAL SCORE

ALIGNING MELODY, HARMONY,
AND RHYTHM IN YOUR BUSINESS

William Stieber, PhD

THE FINAL SCORE
ALIGNING MELODY, HARMONY, AND RHYTHM IN YOUR BUSINESS

iUniverse books may be ordered through booksellers or by contacting:

iUniverse
1663 Liberty Drive
Bloomington, IN 47403
www.iuniverse.com
1-800-Authors (1-800-288-4677)

ISBN: 978-1-5320-3825-9 (sc)
ISBN: 978-1-5320-3824-2 (e)

Library of Congress Control Number: 2017919327

Print information available on the last page.

iUniverse rev. date: 04/16/2018

To my family: Loretta, Jeff, Michael, Michelle, and Olive
And many professional colleagues for their inspiration

CONTENTS

PRELUDE

I WAS IN ELEMENTARY SCHOOL when I was first struck with the beauty and excitement of music. I learned how to play the clarinet and played Ravel's *Bolero* in my early tryouts for a chair in the orchestra. I was stricken with the music bug and later learned how to sing a cappella, to play tenor saxophone, and also what I consider today a respectable bass guitar. In fact, learning music helped defray some of my expenses while attending college. I played in a wedding band, which generated enough income to motivate me to return home several times in my two final years of undergraduate school to play gigs.

As I progressed in the areas of organizational development during my career in leadership development, process improvement, and organizational systems design—and in supporting clients in my own business for the past two decades—I could not help but make connections to my experiences in music.

Developing a sound organization is similar to developing, arranging, and executing a superb musical score. In fact, I even use the terms *melody*, *harmony*, and *rhythm* to describe three critical areas of organizational success to my clients.

I equate melody with the distinct sound and direction provided by leadership in creating or recreating a sound organization. Some leaders are simply great conductors. They provide vision and direction to an organization and can turn a barely surviving organization into a thriving institution with a pleasing sound to its customers, employees, and stakeholders.

When I think of harmony, I often think about my experiences in designing and redesigning organizations. Effective organizations ensure that all their parts are working together collectively. As a result, they provide excellent products and services and delight their customers and their employees. Similarly, a conductor has all the instruments working collaboratively to produce a harmonious outcome. Just as the sections in an orchestra work together to produce a unified passage, effective organizations ensure that their systems and people are aligned in teams so that the right hand knows what the left hand is doing.

Have you ever experienced the dissonance when such alignment fails to exist? The sound is certainly not pleasing to customers. It is not pleasing to the members within the organization. All involved can certainly discern when everyone is not on the same sheet of music.

I have often referred to rhythm as the beat of continuous improvement and change. You can have a great melody and harmony, but if the beat is off, it will sound jarring, antagonistic, and even lethargic. Organizations that have great rhythm keep that beat going. They are never satisfied with just a designed score or a blended system. They know that the environment changes along with customers' needs and tastes. They know they must stay competitive, manage change, and continually improve their products and services or fall off the Fortune 500 list—as many other firms have in the past. They need to stay on the cusp of innovation and use technology and other environmental forces to their advantage. Just being satisfied with a score without rearranging, practicing, or fine-tuning it is unheard of for a performer, a band, or an orchestra if it is going to be recognized among the many organizations competing for the attention of audiences. Organizations need to keep that steady beat of improvement and change to survive in the present and thrive in the future. Managing change and accelerating the rhythm are critical in keeping everyone on the same sheet of music.

Scoring big can be a great challenge. Developing a great melody, harmony, and rhythm in your organization, however, can be your passage to success now and in the future. This book provides guidance for your organization so that you can orchestrate a pleasing sound and score. The result will be music to the ears of many. So grab your baton and follow the bouncing ball through this symphonic journey to success.

Intensify the Melody

THE MELODY IS THAT SINGLE melodic tone that people remember about a musical piece. As mentioned in the prelude, it is often equivalent to the distinct sound that an organization leaves with it customers, employees, and stakeholders. As also mentioned, leadership can have a great hand in creating and intensifying the melody. Often, by intensifying the melody, we are sharpening and making the sound stronger and more succinct. As you review the chapters that follow, remember the word *intensify*. In terms of our musical analogy, it simply represents the following:

- Incorporating innovative changes
- Nourishing customer satisfaction
- Taking the time to satisfy stakeholders
- Ensuring that values are aligned

- **N**ever take your eyes off the music, keeping alert to your environment.
- **S**taying in touch with your audience
- **I**ntegrating opportunities to reinforce direction
- **F**ocusing on retaining winning talent
- **Y**earning for customer and competitive data

These words will take on additional meaning as we progress through this section and the final score.

Is It the Right Key?

In fine-tuning an organization's melody, we want to ensure that we stay in tune with our customers.

The combination of two disagreeing signals—between what is delivered and what the customers want—causes dissonance. In today's social media environment, customers should be involved in the critical feedback processes to minimize unpleasant sounds.

Often a key change of some sort will create added interest for your audiences when playing a sheet of music. Adding variety to your products or services will create that same interest and delight customers. Oftentimes, these adjustments—just like key changes—can be subtle. A slight modification of the design or color or a different service application can add value for customers and create an entirely new set of customers.

Making those key changes, however, requires maintaining an external focus on the audience. It requires that top leaders assume more strategic roles, get out of their organizations, and scan the environments for changing preferences, technology trends, and lifestyle changes. It requires that organizations benchmark externally by conducting visits or making diligent reviews of professional journals and literature for best practices and other methods of making their businesses more efficient and effective.

Key changes can have dramatic effect on your audiences

and customers. They require constant diligence and action in a competitive environment.

Melodic Meditation 1 - Incorporate innovative changes by proactively scanning and benchmarking for best practices and new ideas.

- How are you currently benchmarking external forces?
- Can you improve your current benchmarking practices?
- How do you apply what is learned from benchmarking?
- How is benchmarking part of your ongoing value system?

A Distinctive Sound

An artist playing or singing often tries to be creative to be perceived as unique and exclusive to others. As with a musician with its audience, developing attractiveness with customers is also a desire of high-performing organizations.

Organizations develop such distinctiveness, as does the musician, by paying attention to providing quality products and services and by adding unique features to their offerings to pleasantly surprise and delight their customers. As a customer, I was pleasantly surprised by the addition of frequent-flier points when traveling. After some time, customers, including myself, expected them as more and more airlines started offering such add-ons to their passengers' travel packages.

Several years ago, I received a phone call soon after checking into my hotel room. The voice at the other end of the phone said, "Hello, Dr. Stieber. Is everything satisfactory with your room and check-in?" It was a delight to be asked. How great is it to show concern for a customer almost immediately following arrival? What can your organization do to add such features to your products and services on an ongoing basis?

Organizations such as 3M provide time for employees to be creative. What can you do on a consistent basis to capture the creative and innovative thoughts of talent in your organization? Do you have the right culture and values to support innovation? What processes, systems or virtual options do you have in place to create new ideas? Have you really fostered the right environment so that employees will offer their creative thoughts?

Leaders can also help create distinctiveness. Reinforcing a positive work climate, reinforcing creative and innovative ideas, and allowing input and questioning by staff members sets the foundation for promoting innovation.

Melodic Meditation 2 - Nourish customer satisfaction by looking for ways to surprise your customers with unique products, services, and other customer-focused actions.

- What have you done to surprise customers with unique products or services?
- Does the organization provide leadership for employees, creating an innovative environment?
- How does your organization reinforce creative ideas for employees?

Ensuring the Right Dynamics

Dynamics refer to the musical notations that a performer may review that demonstrate how loudly or softly to play certain notes or phrases. At times, leaders can create dynamics that will help an organization provide good melodies, whether it is to trumpet loud sounds, often referred to as f (forte) in music, or to orchestrate softer tones, noted as p (piano) in music. Creating the right dynamics will build commitment by adopting and applying subtle yet enduring actions in an organization.

Organizations that recognize that there are other outcomes associated with the community and corporate social responsibility beyond the bottom line can really set themselves apart from businesses that are interested only in the bottom line. These activities, whether it is involving employees in projects for Habitat for Humanity or simply making a donation to the local community center, need to be emphasized and projected by the organization and its leadership.

Less pronounced activities that provide employees the right type of culture and recognize a balanced work life locally can serve as a quiet distinction to employees who make the organization a preferred employer in its industry. Providing flexible hours or workplaces to respond to the new working generation of millennials' need for wellness can only add to an organization's attractiveness and retention levels.

Melodic Meditation 3 - Take time to satisfy stakeholders in unique ways by assuming social responsibility and providing opportunities for balance in your workforce.

- What has your organization done to reach out to the community? To other stakeholders?
- What actions has the organization taken to support employee wellness?
- Does your organization's culture support a balanced work life? If not, what changes can be made?

Creating a Pleasing Sound

Once the strategy is in place, it is important to maintain that mission and vision and communicate that ideal state along with the organization's purpose.

One difference I notice in truly successful organizations is the sustainment of values. These values have implications for those working in the organization and spillover to the customers during employee interactions. In some organizations, you may notice a set of values displayed on the wall and communicated in an annual report or newsletter. Truly excellent organizations go beyond the typical rhetoric on values and institutionalize them as an integral way of living and acting within and outside a company.

State-of-the-art leaders look for key communication opportunities to integrate the values in everything an organization does. They typically are included in key orientation and training processes and are reinforced in key celebrations and communications. Leaders who really make a difference in the sound an organization makes internally and externally look for opportunities to reinforce and sustain the values over time.

A financial-services organization involved in a large ticket credit-lending business I supported included an annual 360-degree feedback process for all leaders—from the top of the organization to the very bottom ranks of leaders. This 360-degree feedback process was strictly focused on how well the leaders were living the values in their organizations. I had to provide the CEO with feedback on how well he was perceived to be living the values by his direct reports. It could have been a terrifying experience, but the CEO was an enlightened leader and accepted the feedback openly. He agreed to work on key actions going forward. His direct reports also provided great support to the process and openly accepted the feedback. It is no wonder that this business surpassed many of the others in financial results stemming from customer and employee satisfaction. The leader was focused on both the culture and the strategy, which helped the organization maintain a true melody that was pleasing to the customers and the employees, positively impacting the profitability of the business unit.

Values stated are important for creating a pleasing sound. Values driven by innovation and flexibility are pleasing to the customer, helping set the tone for the right behaviors in driving a customer-focused organization.

Evaluating customers' experiences are as important as getting feedback from your audiences. Having a system for review is an important ongoing effort that organizations need to incorporate so that they know when their products or services are getting stale and are no longer pleasing to the customer. Secure ideas for improvement—just like musicians secure feedback on their performances. Having customer-focused values is one thing, but living those values and incorporating periodic feedback to ensure they are reinforced is equally important.

Melodic Meditation 4 - Ensure that values are aligned to create positive customer expectations.

- What values might help drive the right behaviors for your business?
- How might you improve how you communicate those values?
- Is employee feedback part of your daily processes?

Maintaining Intonation

Sometimes we hear an orchestra play flat or sharp, but an organization that wants to stay in tune needs to adjust to an ever-changing set of environmental forces and customer needs. Just like musicians need to adjust periodically and check to ensure they are in tune, so do groups and systems within an organization. By periodically revisiting forces, surveying customers' changing needs and trends, and assessing processes for efficiency and effectiveness, the sound can remain pleasant to both stakeholders and customers.

Melodic Meditation 5 - Never take your eyes off the sheet music, Keep alert to the environment and conduct periodic surveys for assessment and adjustment.

- What types of surveys have you conducted to assess your operations?
- How have you explored needs and trends that may impact the products and services you offer to the marketplace?
- How have you assessed your effectiveness in a changing environment to meet stakeholder preferences?

Understanding the Audience

Melody is the succession of single tones in musical compositions, as distinguished from harmony and rhythm or a rhythmical succession of single tones producing a distinct musical phrase or idea.

When an organization wants to produce a distinct sound that is pleasing to its customers, employees, or other stakeholders, it must work on the tones that will resonate and provide a distinct advantage that sets it apart from others. This is often launched with a good strategy that includes your mission, vision, key goals, objectives, and values that help make your organization known for great products and services and as an employer of choice.

Organizations that become entities of excellence often scan their environments to gain an understanding of their audiences' current and future needs. With audiences looking for more visual stimulation along with music, we see musical organizations such as Cirque du Soleil changing their venues to meet these changing needs. Progressive organizations frequently do such external scans to remain in touch with their customers' current needs and to anticipate future needs as well. This practice helps an organization peak their audience's interest causing them to pay attention.

Melodic Meditation 6 - Stay in touch with your audience to increase your understanding.

- What would you describe as your audience's current needs?
- How would you characterize your distinct sound? What advantage will you be giving your customers?
- How will you remain in touch with your customers as a means of anticipating future needs?

Staying in Tune and Minimizing Dissonance

Most musical groups tune up their instruments prior to their concerts. They make sure they are in tune after the beginning of the concerts, during key parts of the concerts, and during intermissions. These constant adjustments ensure that they continue their performances while staying in tune with their ensembles of musicians. In spite of that, clashing intervals or chords occur, which may be very unpleasant to the audience. Often, it is a purposely written part in an arrangement. This same type of dissonance can often be noted in an organization. It is often noted in an inconsistency between one's actions and one's beliefs.

Staying in tune is important for creating the right type of culture and minimizing contention in the workforce. Ultimately, the right organizational culture helps build customer loyalty and improve business results. Unfortunately, employees can experience conflict when an organization's values indicate the importance of teamwork but management rewards individual efforts.

An organization might have quality slogans and efforts throughout the enterprise and be more concerned about shipping or delivering on schedule than quality and safety. Another organization may say it values communication but only be interested in reporting good news so numbers are manipulated or decisions are made based on agreement with leadership more than on valid data or facts. This can ultimately lead to higher employee turnover, resulting in increased human capital costs for the organization. Such challenges may also be created by internal issues associated with broken-down processes when the left hand does not know what the right hand is doing, thereby creating a clashing image for the customer or audience.

An organization can minimize such dissonance via consistency between values and actions. A large telecommunications and financial organization, which I supported as an organizational design and development consultant, found creative ways to influence behaviors that drove the organization's values. The financial organization ensured that its organizational values were ingrained into as many initiatives and processes as possible. They were part of a handbook given to all employees and were included in major presentations and training initiatives whenever possible. These tools helped reduce discord and provided a better work environment, which ultimately increased customer satisfaction and financial results.

Creating a process that focuses on team-based approaches to delivering products and services can minimize the latter type of dissonance. You can also minimize dissonance by creating a customer-oriented culture. Rewarding customer-focused behavior by hiring the right people and reinforcing customer-focused behaviors is a great start. Getting the whole organization involved in customer-focused activities and establishing trust and great communication lines in that pursuit also adds value to such focus.

Melodic Meditation 7 - Integrate opportunities to reinforce the right values in your organization Maximize the process by eliminating functional silos.

- What have you done to instill a team approach in the organization?
- Is team culture part of the daily focus and process?
- Does the team approach ensure a quicker and more effective response to customers and stakeholders?

Hitting the High Notes to Success

There are often challenges in musical scores. As a musician, it was a challenge to play high notes while staying in tune. Sustaining notes and hitting high notes requires a lot of breath support. Organizations often have those same challenges and they often appear once success is attained. The problem is not always developing a competitive business but maintaining that business over a long period of time.

Organizations and leaders first need to focus on retaining winning talent. Too often, organizations have focused on the recruiting and selection of talent. The key to hitting those high notes to success is focusing on developing human capital. Organizations remain competitive by putting succession plans in place so that they can develop the high potentials and key successors of the future.

Proactive plans can be developed to retain the best-in-class employees who are important to the organization's mission and vision by assessing the vulnerability of the organization and identifying key leadership and technical positions that could potentially depart from the organization. Savvy clients are keen on developing retention plans prior to major reorganizations, outsourcing efforts, or other changes so they do not lose the winning talent in their organizations.

Establishing learning cultures where learning is valued and shared by all can also drive success. An organization I once supported had a motto of "Shared Skills, Shared Success." After completion of a project or completion of a major learning event, individuals or teams would schedule presentations so that any member of the organization could learn about individual or group key learning successes or challenges associated with a key learning event.

Hitting those high notes to success also involves maintaining competitive processes and constantly reevaluating your organization's designs that engage employees so it is truly proactive in responding to your changing customer needs and environmental forces.

One organization I supported would constantly reevaluate its strategy plans, operational plans, and designs. After surveying customers and reviewing processes, the organizations determined that its customers were only concerned about company response and representative contact. The organization was able to implement regional offices and close many local offices, which resulted in employees working out of their homes. The change increased customer and employee satisfaction and significantly reduced operating expenses.

Melodic Meditation 8 - Focus on retaining winning talent, particularly during times of change.

- How do you engage talented employees?
- Do you develop retention plans for talented employees that can assist the organization in the future?
- How do you evaluate processes and designs that engage employees while proactively responding to current and future customer and stakeholder needs?

Capturing the Right Voicing

Voicing is the instrumentation, vertical spacing, and ordering of the pitches in a chord and the determination of instruments or voices that perform each. Once you have current customer information and identify external forces being faced, you can gain a better perception of what products and services might be pleasing to those customers and identify the order or sequence of how to best deliver those products and services. Timing is everything, and we will review that later in relationship to an organization's rhythm. Launching your strategy—including key goals and objectives—can be critically based on customer needs and other forces, including noise from your competitors.

Melodic Meditation 9 - Yield to customers and competitive data to find the right clues and implement the most effective timing for your goals and objectives.

- How do you accumulate and maintain customer information?
- How might you regularly assess information for business implications?
- How do you connect your implementation efforts to critical times and issues associated with customer needs?

DESIGN THE HARMONY

WHILE MELODY INVOLVES SINGLE TONES, when I think of harmony, I think of chords. Harmony is the combination or the blending of tones that are pleasing to the ear. Whether it is a barbershop quartet, a symphony orchestra, or a contemporary band, the introduction of harmony adds so much to a piece of music. Consider these actions as you add your harmony:

- Design the organization so it can sustain itself.
- Ensure that you reinforce the strategy.
- Seek the continuous-improvement beat.
- Integrate all elements of the support system.
- Gain alignment by paying attention to values and principles.
- Navigate so that you organize around processes.

These points will be elaborated on as you review some of the next pages and the "Harmonic Hints" provided in this section and in the final score.

Rhapsody of Sustainability

The term *sustainability* has increased in popularity. In music, it often implies something that is free in form and expression. While you may think about it in terms of environment or social challenges, I often think of the term as the capacity to endure. Organizations need to think about the notion of sustainability on many fronts. The idea of sustainable development in the future has garnered great interest among consumers, stakeholders, and employees. Some research supports that sustainability of products and services can attract and motivate customers to purchase goods and services from an organization.

An organization needs to create its *analysis system stage*, a free-form design that helps it sustain itself in the future. A built-in system that reassesses and redesigns the organization on a regular basis requires planning for sustainability. The plan could include changes to culture, processes, and a host of other parts, as well as reviewing goals and objectives on an ongoing basis and keeping records of progress. It would be analogous to the old Deming model of improvement (plan, do, check, act).

One financial organization I supported would establish renewal teams so that, after some organizational design was implemented, they evaluated the success of the design to ensure that the organization was progressing as planned and implemented any actions necessary to sustain that design in the future. Ongoing efforts to assess whether efforts are connecting with customers and other forces to ensure sustainability in the future are critical if an organization is going to stay ahead of its competition and continue to be a recognized name.

Harmonic Hint 1 - Design the organization so that it can sustain itself.

- What have you done to integrate sustainability into your products or services?
- Do you present an image of sustainability to your customers?
- How have you reached out to your customer base by emphasizing sustainability?

Everyone under the Same Direction

While a melody can often be accomplished by one musician, harmony always involves several notes and several musicians. When there are several musicians involved, it is important that the ensemble plays together so that the overall chords are executed to perfection. This means that each individual must execute his or her part correctly, release notes, articulate dynamics, and reenter the score at the same time. This often takes practice and hard work.

Organizations often have a similar challenge. They have different departments and personnel all making individual contributions toward a final product or service in their organizational roles. Getting everyone on the same page is not always easy. Just like with a music group, working together takes practice and hard work to ensure a pleasing sound for your customers. An organization where the right hand does not know what the left hand is doing often results in disharmony and chaos and leaves a poor impression on customers.

At the top of the organization, you need to create a compelling mission, vision, and set of values. It must be reinforced and reiterated as much as possible. This strategic action is an initial, critical step in ensuring that people are moving in the same direction.

An organization involved in the insurance and health care arena developed teams to work on the organization's values and worked with the executive team to develop a compelling strategy. The strategy was successful because they developed a great communication strategy so that the leadership could reinforce the values as frequently as opportunities surfaced. They also found ways through performance management and training systems to reinforce values and other important elements of the strategy periodically to ensure constant exposure in the organization.

Having good visible processes and procedures so that everyone is sure of what their roles are can be very beneficial. Some of my clients have disassembled their functional organizations and moved toward a more process-focused organization. People have more clarity about the steps and their roles in the workflows and in terms of how they fit in the processing of an organization's product or service.

Harmonic Hint 2 - Ensure that you reinforce the strategy and institutionalize key values and components that support the strategy.

- What values and guiding principles have you reinforced to ensure the right behaviors are driving your strategy?
- What has been done to ensure employee roles are clear, minimizing confusion for the customer?
- Are all parts of the organization on the same page?

The Beat of Continuous Improvement

Whether you call it *Total Quality Management, Six Sigma,* or *Lean Six Sigma,* or use of the Baldrige criteria, organizations that really are interested in developing a sound rhythm make a serious effort to improve and continue efforts to never be satisfied with the status quo. They look to continue to improve their processes both internally and externally so that they continue to refine their processes to ensure sustainability. They should implement and improve measures that focus on the voice of the customer. This often requires the organization to listen to the key information regarding customer requirements and needs. Unfortunately, organizations often have weak of *voice of the customer systems.*

Effective organizations continue to refine their strategic actions, metrics, and information systems so they have the critical items in place to achieve their strategies and prioritize real customer knowledge. They ensure balance by focusing on the customer and employee development and satisfaction. As opposed to organizations that use a quality initiative simply as a checklist, they measure the results as well to ensure they are getting a good return on their investment in such initiatives.

I had a short assignment with a global automobile enterprise, and a worker was going through what appeared to be calisthenics or an exercise tryout. He was merely trying to refine the process of how a worker might go about adding a part to an automobile in the production line in a more ergonomically sound way that was less likely to cause injury or stress. Such examples demonstrate the degree to which some organizations take improvement seriously.

Organizations that want to secure that steady beat also continuously look for ways to improve their results. Just as a meter change in rhythm can occur abruptly in a piece of music, organizations need to adapt to sudden change. Typically, those results are related to a number of different areas associated with their success and alignment. They often include financial results, customer results, employee engagement, and turnover results, along with other stakeholder areas associated with alignment and ultimately success.

Harmonic Hint 3 - Seek the continuous-improvement beat that helps sustain organizational effectiveness and efficiency by measuring all critical result areas of your operations.

- What customer metrics have you integrated into your organization's measurement systems?
- What metrics have you used to measure human capital investment?
- What other opportunities exist beyond the financial measures to assess the success of your organization?

Do You Have the Right Accompaniment?

We have often heard vocalists without instrumental accompaniment. These groups, which are often associated with the oldies or barbershop quartets, sound pleasing. With instrumental accompaniment, there is quite a pleasant sound. There can be a great string section, but one hears such a more robust sound when it is accompanied by brass, woodwind, and percussion sections. An organization needs to have a strategy in place that includes a vision, mission, goals, and values to create a pleasing sound. The operational systems that support such a vision must be in place in order to accomplish and make the overall strategy robust in nature.

You can think of it as the necessary ingredients to a great concert!

You first need to think about the *player system*. Just like with a band or an orchestra, you must recruit, hire, train, and retain the best talent to accomplish and sustain your organization. Having the best and brightest players can help you maintain a competitive organization. Today, more organizations are concentrating on the retention issue after realizing the extreme costs of turnover associated with finding the right talent and then losing it.

You next need to think about the *applause system*. Just as a group of musicians thrives on the applause from the audience, employees also love recognition. Developing both formal and informal rewards to retain key players can be a ticket to success for your organization. You can increase retention by noticing your employees.

One of the categories in a rubric for evaluation of a musical group is known as the *organization system*. Such a system is also necessary for any effective company in designing itself to accomplish its goals. Having a good structure in today's competitive climate is critical when delivering quality products and services in a prompt and easy-to-do business way. Many companies have eliminated many of the layers associated with the bureaucracies of the past and used teams as a way to structure themselves so they can be quick and nimble in responding to customers' needs.

The most significant structure changes have supported and included self-managed teams. These teams often operate independently, proceeding daily without much direction from the outside. In several instances, they evaluate each other within the team. They are typically rewarded based on team success. Such empowered structures have led to performance success and high measures of accomplishment.

Any good musician needs a good *notation system* so that the notes are clearly documented to perform and execute a great score. Such information systems are also necessary in organizations. How information is stored, accessed, and made available can certainly impact an organization's performance just as the score itself can be an important component in influencing the overall performance by musicians and the reaction from the audience.

You may have great values associated with customer focus and even a great reward system that positively rewards customer-satisfaction behaviors, but if you do not have good information systems available so that employees can access data quickly and execute customer service and solve customer problems promptly, the impact of the other factors may be minimal in terms of overall results. An example of an effective information system today being used is the customer-relationship management (CRM) system. Your name may be a part of such a system without you even knowing it. If you have purchased an automobile or have had a car repaired, your name is often integrated into such a system.

Having such systems can often lead companies to securing lifetime customers, which can have a major impact on an organization's long-term bottom line.

When a conductor and a group of musicians put their mark on a musical score, it is often referred to as an interpretation of their own adaptation of a particular piece of music. This *interpretation system* is also needed as the organization's tasks are accomplished. With such interpretation, clear decision-making roles need to be notated so that the organization's tasks are performed with efficiency and effectiveness.

A good performance is impacted by the role of the conductor, performers, soloists, and a host of others. Any uncertainty of roles can impact the ultimate performance. A collaborative approach with clarity and cohesiveness can only effectively be experienced when all the key areas understand their roles and expectations of one another. This also is true in other organizations. Each significant part of an organization's structure needs to clearly understand its role in accomplishing its mission and goals. At a smaller organizational level, I often use a role-and-responsibility matrix to clarify roles of the key parts of the organization and clearly define the key support roles. It does wonders for effectiveness and efficiency and often reduces bureaucracy and chaos. Customers certainly recognize when all parts of an organization are working well together.

Having the right equipment and location is important to any performance. Organizations need to consider the *performance system* as well. Having the right policies, procedures, and facilities to produce products and services most effectively is as critical to an organization as it is to a musical group that is making a recording or completing a live performance. After all, if your need for teams is critical to increasing responsiveness to customers, organizing your office space in pods may be more effective than lined cubicles.

In one team-based organization I supported, they rearranged

the team so they could see each other and respond to phone calls from any work location. Being responsive to customer calls was an important component of the organization's values and productivity. The right use of facilities and correct arrangements helps produce positive results. Can you imagine a percussion section seated at the front of an orchestra or band for the entire concert?

Finally, an *analysis system* that ensures that the organization is constantly fine-tuning itself is critical to an organization's survival and sustainability. Some of the greatest orchestras are great because they are constantly practicing and finding new and creative ways to perform for audiences. The constant review and evaluation—followed by the fine-tuning of systems and approaches—ensures an organization's continued appearance in the Fortune 500. Without such rigor, an organization is likely to lose customer focus and competitiveness.

Input	Process	Feedback
	Player System	
	Organization System	
Applause System	Notation System	Analysis System
	Interpretation System	
	Performance System	

Harmonic Hint 4 - Integrate all elements of your support system.

- What have you done to ensure an effective and efficient structure, minimizing costs and maximizing customer satisfaction?
- Are your performance systems in place to create the right impact?

- What have you done to make evaluation a repetitive process so that your organization sustains success over time?

Concert Manners

When you go to a concert, there are certain types of behaviors and manners that must be adhered to, depending on the type of concert you attend.

When ensuring alignment, it is important that an organization be clear about what behaviors are expected of both new and experienced members of the organization. If the organization succeeds in this endeavor, people know what behaviors are critical to the organization's success. If not clear, the organization can be dysfunctional. Competing behaviors will get in the way of the organization accomplishing its mission and vision.

An effective way that I have seen to ensure that all employees are headed in the right direction is having values or *guiding principles.* If organizations have strategic directions they are trying to accomplish, they must determine the attitudes, behaviors, and skills that will drive them to accomplish their goals, objectives, and strategies.

For instance, if an increase in customer satisfaction is required to attain productivity and market outcomes, key values around being nimble and responsive to customer needs might be critical.

It is important to develop those values, but the organization and its leadership must have processes in place to operationalize them, including recruiting and performance-management training. When leaders and employees are modeling such values—with the right manners in place—they can they accomplish what the organization and its leaders want.

Teams are an important part of many organizations today. If team behaviors are critical, those collaborative behaviors must be rewarded and included as part of the organization's values.

You cannot be team based when you are hiring and looking for entrepreneurial behaviors in potential candidates.

Harmonic Hint 5 - Gain alignment by paying attention to values and principles supporting important behaviors and attitudes.

- Are the skills, behaviors, and expectations of employees developed to align with your strategic goals?
- Have you evaluated the team, ensuring the organizational direction?
- What changes in your organization need to be made to ensure strategic alignment?

Blending the Ensembles

Organizations that value teamwork typically are more successful in developing harmony and producing seamless processes for customers. There is less bureaucracy and red tape in dealing with those organizations. Customers see such organizations as easy to do business with because they ensure that their processes are efficient and effective in meeting customer requirements. They reinforce the values of customer focus as part of their culture, and they reward teamwork. Many organizations say they do this, but they fail to because of their individually focused reward systems. Others use their values as important criteria for recruiting and selecting team players and developing customer-focused skills and knowledge.

As a leader, it is important to recruit members who have already worked in teams and customer-focused organizations. When actually interviewing, effective organizations include questions pertaining to attitudes concerning teams and actual behaviors in situations displaying customer-focused behaviors. Some organizations use customer-service competencies and behavioral interviewing techniques to ensure that they are hiring the most qualified candidates that best fit their culture.

Another important characteristic of effective blending in an organization is giving leaders the right tools for blending the ensemble of workers. They organize around processes and ensure that all players know how they fit into the overall picture. They take the necessary time to use tools to ensure that all players know their roles and responsibilities on key tasks and projects associated with taking the organization to the next level.

They foster an environment of shared skills and shared success. The lack of connection often associated with remoteness is removed when all parts of the organization share successes with other parts of the organization. This constant mode of development helps with the blending process.

Harmonic Hint 6 - **N**avigate so that you organize around processes. Ensure that team and customer values serve as a foundation for hiring, reinforcement, and reward systems.

- Have leaders been given the right tools to create a cohesive team?
- Are your values incorporated as integral screening criteria in your selection and recruitment process?
- How do you assess customer focus and team behaviors? How do you reward them?

ACCELERATE THE RHYTHM

A third critical factor associated with scoring big and securing alignment is rhythm. When I think of rhythm, I think about important elements of music: beat, tempo, and the general pattern or pulses associated with time, accent, or meter.

"I Got Rhythm" is an old tune from my early days as a musician. Unfortunately, I find that some organizations have poor rhythm—or no rhythm at all. Poor rhythm can be observed as a slow, lethargic tempo that is associated with producing delayed responses to customer needs or customer complaints. The source could be from an overabundance of bureaucracy and slow decision making, which is often associated with multiple layers of structure, lack of defined processes to get things done, or poorly outlined roles and responsibilities.

Organizations, on the other hand, can develop exciting,

invigorating, and aligned rhythm by following a few simple steps to accelerate the rhythm:

- Add large-scale organizational design
- Combine leadership reinforcement
- Continue to look at internal components and external forces
- Engage people in strategy advancement, technology change and innovation
- Look for ways to provide time and reinforce creativity
- Ensure that leaders are a key part of the communication plan
- Reinforce positive values that focus on retaining winning talent
- Accept feedback and proactively collecting information
- Target customer with positive surprises
- Elicit leadership in taking key roles in reinforcing behaviors

These actions will be reinforced and expanded on the following pages and in the final score.

Inserting the Movement

EXPANDING PROCESS IMPROVEMENT TO A larger scale through the review of cultural values, strategy, and operational choices made by the organization can be exhilarating and invigorating. As with any musical movement that is an extension of an existing work, large-scale change is merely an extension of any improvement initiatives associated with alignment and scoring big as an enterprise. It adds to the rhythm and ongoing heartbeat, which are important for the organization's survival and sustainability.

Facilitating redesign teams was one of my more thrilling experiences as an organizational development practitioner. It allowed some of the best and brightest to be involved in designing major systems for their organization. It was quite exciting to facilitate design teams and leaders while integrating new business units into the total operation. It was also rewarding to watch the learning and the engagement going on throughout the design and implementation phases. Allowing such improvement extensions can significantly decrease the large-scale redesigns, which are often required when an organization has been lax at improving itself. It can also significantly increase financial, customer, and employee results.

Rhythmic Reflection 1 - Add large-scale organizational redesign efforts to maximize results.

- What change efforts has your organization taken to assess your current state of business?
- What studies have you conducted to scan your environment, internal processes, and social implications associated with your strategy?
- What comprehensive design approaches have you used that impact all organizational systems supporting your strategy?

Executing Allegro and Minimizing Adagio

In music, I always enjoyed the brisk tempo of *allegro*, which can be challenging for a musician from an execution standpoint due to the difficulty in fingering the keys. There were at times however, where the slow tempo of *adagio* provided a great contrast.

In executing that briskness and crisp allegro tempo, an organization can set itself up for success within the swift and changing environments companies move within today. It has to have all the previously mentioned systems working together in harmony so that behaviors, processes, technology, structure, and the performance system are directed toward accomplishing the goals and moving the organization forward in its competitive landscape.

To operate effectively, leadership needs to reinforce the strategy and values that support the systems in place. You can tell when an organization is operating at an allegro tempo because there is an urgency to satisfy customers and a commitment to provide efficient and effective processes in meeting customer needs. There is also a rhythm where each function effectively partners in support of each other, and the superordinate goals of the enterprise as a whole work together to ensure that the end result is a quality one with profitability in order to sustain the organization.

There is sometimes a need for adagio. This is often the time when the organization takes a time-out to study lessons learned and engage in the analysis phase. Some reflection time is required to identify successes, identify gaps that need improvement, and implement actions to improve the organization's design and processes to sustain success. Once these actions are in place, the organization should work on streamlining its workflows and processes to return to the exciting, fast-paced allegro tempo, which can only serve to improve its customer base and maintain a loyal workforce.

Rhythmic Reflection 2 - Combine leadership reinforcement and team collaboration to quicken the tempo, but take a time-out to reflect on learning to sustain success.

- What have you done to ensure internal communication and leadership reinforcement of your key messages and strategy?
- How often do you reflect on lessons learned and incorporate them into new strategies and actions?
- When was the last time your processes were reviewed?

Optimizing the Pieces

For a future of greatness, we need to develop organizations that can adjust and adapt themselves to fulfill their obligations. We need to ensure that multiple entities are coordinated in a fashion to accomplish the organization's strategies in an effective and efficient manner.

Just as a conductor emphasizes certain sections or instruments in an orchestra, leaders need to design their organizations and look systemically at data. In addition to examining external customers, stakeholders, and environmental forces for implications of how to proceed, they need to look at their workflows and processes to ensure alignment with their strategies. They also need to look at the member surveys and ensure that their designs address human capital needs.

Appropriate redesigns of the organization need to consider external issues, process and workflow issues, and people issues so that the organization is moving aligned in the same direction to accomplish goals in an effective and efficient manner while also keeping an eye on sustainability.

Rhythmic Reflection 3 - Continue to examine all internal components and external forces to affect the organization to stay in tune and redesign for greatness.

- Are there any improvement opportunities in your processes that merit review and change?
- What external forces have been considered in your strategy? Can any changes impact what and how you deliver to your customers?
- Are any internal or external problems decreasing effectiveness?

Tremolo of Excitement

One of the most interesting sounds I have heard when playing in musical ensembles has been the exciting sound created by the *tremolo*. Tremolo is considered the rapid reiteration of a single sound or single chord in music. I have always enjoyed the sound of a banjo in the groups I have played with. When they performed a tremolo on the banjo, it has added variety, excitement, and a great vibrating effect to the music. The quick back-and-forth motion associated with playing a tremolo on the banjo can also add to the entertainment value of the selection—whether it is with a ragtime band or other ensemble.

Organizations can generate that same level of excitement by performing that quick back-and-forth motion to continually align their processes with their strategies. The greatest advances in technology and other innovations were identified by projected customer needs (based on external data-collection efforts). Organizations can minimize the resistance that often comes with such change by counteracting that resistance with commitment. In gaining commitment, it helps to identify key actions that need to be deployed to overcome and manage resistance so that a specific change during such actions has a great opportunity to succeed.

We are creatures of habit. Change often brings resistance. Organizations can minimize such resistance by working on increasing the levels of commitment. One of the tools I often use—and encourage my clients to use—is a stakeholder-commitment plan. This forces organizations to identify stakeholders associated with a change and develop influence strategies to increase the commitment to the necessary level for changes to succeed.

By getting all involved in these efforts, it becomes a fabric of the organization. And by becoming an interwoven piece of the organization's culture, this tremolo effect is realized by the entire organization. With such realization, the tune of "We've Got Rhythm" is realized. Such involvement is likely to increase employee engagement and satisfaction while decreasing the organization's turnover costs. This excitement can also have a positive impact on productivity and a tremendous impact on attracting the type of talent and human capital an organization needs to compete and become a top hit in its industry.

Rhythmic Reflection 4 - Engage people in strategy advancement, technological change, and innovation. Maintain a tremolo of satisfaction with engagement.

- What barriers within the organization's infrastructure limit employee engagement?
- What opportunities within the organization develop employee commitment?
- Does your organization attract outside personnel looking to join the team?

Allowing for Improvisation

I have always enjoyed playing with contemporary groups or participating in jazz jam sessions where people were judged on how they played and how they *improvised*. I always felt a sense of accomplishment when what I put together by winging it met the mark of acceptance. I also felt a great deal of delight when my colleagues were developing some unforeseen passage based on imagination or creativity.

Organizations often need to improvise and are often cited for their ability to improvise in responding to customers or providing some unique and creative solution to a need in the marketplace. The most intriguing organizations are often those that devise solutions to requirements in the absence of the resources one might typically expect would be needed in specific scenarios. Many things have to happen in order to create the right type of environment so that such improvisation takes place.

Members of the organization must be willing to take some risks at times. Leaders need to create the right types of environments so that mistakes are tolerated and appropriate risk-taking is rewarded. This also means that some of the behaviors reinforced in an organization's culture include creativity and innovation.

Organizations need to create time for improvisation. Many organizations provide some time for their members to be creative and innovative. They provide time during the daily workday for employees to help the organization develop more creative products, services, and ways of doing work. Organizations that value such improvisation can see the impact of such dedication of time to creativity. These organizations will be successful, and they will sustain themselves in the future.

Culture, leadership behaviors, reward systems, and performance systems all need to be aligned for such improvisation to benefit the organization. The side benefit of this approach is employee engagement and retention.

Rhythmic Reflection 5 - Look for ways to provide time and reinforce creativity and innovation in the organization.

- How do leaders in your organization typically respond to mistakes?
- How would you assess the level of risk-taking in your organization? Is this assessment where it should be to remain competitive?
- How is improvisation rewarded in your organization? Do employees feel safe enough to improvise?

Creating the Fanfare

We often hear an orchestra or band play some fanfare. It often involves a loud flourish of brass instruments, and it is often played at a ceremonial event. Creating such fanfare is often important for establishing the right tempo and rhythm in the organization.

A spectacular public display of support for values that support ongoing improvement, including customer-focused and employee-engagement behaviors, is critical.

Many organizations I have supported have ceremonies for customer focus and/or employee engagement. Typical examples of such fanfare included holding key learning sessions where teams would share improvements and lessons from helpful organizational projects with the entire organization. Executives shared overviews of key customer strategies and results that featured actual customer testimonials. On-the-spot ceremonies and employee publications that described extra efforts to satisfy customers or solve perplexing organizational problems added to the enthusiasm and fanfare.

Rhythmic Reflection 6 - Ensure leaders are a key part of the communication plan—and include organization systems that support improvement.

- What are the required frequency, messages, and methodologies to communicate and create fanfare?
- How are you integrating fanfare into your annual planning process?
- What are some innovative ways you can integrate fanfare to get people excited about the organization's progress and direction?

Dancing the Jig

An organization with rhythm has a resounding liveliness about it. It includes a loyalty where employees are not afraid to sing the organization's praises and make the extra effort to ensure that work is done effectively and efficiently. It is an organization where you see the rhythmic demonstration of commitment and hear the lively accompaniment to daily work. It isn't easy to get everyone dancing the jig. It can be as difficult as creating an environment of improvisation, but many organizations display such liveliness when dealing with employees. It is partly due to the culture developed so that values—and the resulting behaviors that are reinforced—lead to positive results.

The *player system* also contributes to that dramatic effect. If you spend the time recruiting, assessing, and selecting the right talent with the right behaviors, liveliness echoes throughout the organization as it accomplishes its tasks and interacts with customers and stakeholders. Part of the player system focuses on retaining key talent.

Many organizations have spent significant resources to attract and recruit top talent, but fewer organizations have spent the time and resources required to retain that talent. Those that do are dancing the jig and engaging employees who might otherwise be lost to competitors. They are dancing the jig because they realize that they have saved significant dollars that might have been lost in turnover of talent and with hiring and training new employees.

Rhythmic Reflection 7 - Reinforce positive values and focus on retaining winning talent.

- What is the degree of employee loyalty and commitment in your organization? Is it where it should be?
- Does your turnover rate reflect too much cost? What are you doing to change that cost?
- Have you invested in leadership development so that effective skills exist in the areas of talent assessment and development?

Critiquing the Performance

Just as an orchestra member and conductor or another musical group looks for the critic's reviews following a performance, so should leaders of an organization engage in the monitoring and assessment of whether old or new designs are meeting requirements. They should do this on a regular basis. Are the organizational systems all performing and aligned so that they are all doing exactly what owners and stakeholders expect them to do? Are the organizational systems providing clear accountabilities, roles, and structures that support the goals and objectives of the enterprise? Is the player system in place so that the organization is attracting the best and the brightest and retaining them with the right incentives that are essential for success?

Just as an ensemble reviews its critics and feedback, organizations need to look at such alignment and review evaluations, surveys, and complaints for opportunities to improve.

Rhythmic Reflection 8 - Accepting feedback and proactively collecting information will allow the organization to sing from the same sheet music.

- How have you orchestrated feedback so internal suppliers have a chance to consider opportunities to improve on your customer focus?
- Have you established a culture where feedback is welcomed by employees, customers, and suppliers?
- Is feedback an integral part of the ongoing processes in the organization?

Handling the Crescendo and Decrescendo

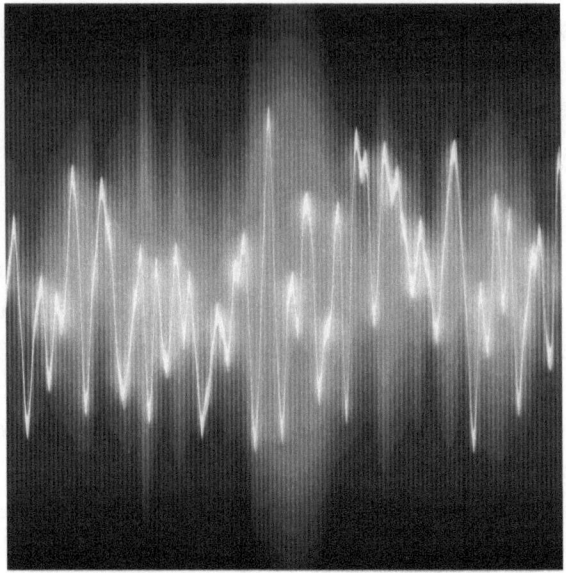

Musical groups and orchestras can create dramatic effects with *dynamics, crescendos* (gradual increases in volume), or *decrescendos* (gradual decreases in volume).

Organizations can also create the same impact that these dynamic changes have and that we hear as audience members. The gradual increases in volume equate to the increases in customer delight and employee satisfaction.

Increases in customer satisfaction are often discovered when a firm catches a customer by surprise with a sudden, unexpected positive delivery in either products or services provided. Such results can often be attained because of a firm's constant attention to continual improvement or large-scale designs aimed to place the firm in a far superior position from a competitive standpoint. It could also result from a firm's ability to focus on innovation and develop unique features associated with its products or services. These delighters often serve to increase satisfaction on a gradual but continuing basis (as noted in my earlier example of the hotel check-in). Organizations that focus on designing such surprises can only crescendo to the point that they remain first-class destinations for customers.

An organization that emphasizes the importance of employees realizes it can enhance retention efforts and serve in enhancing the positive interactions that customers have with their organization's members. Over the past few decades, organizations that focus on employee development and employee engagement have seen reduced costs via reduced turnover and higher worker engagement. When this happens on an ongoing basis, commitment increases gradually to the point that some organizations move from the worst place to work to employers of choice.

A decrescendo can also be very effective with audiences. Moving from a very loud sound to a gradually softer sound during a performance can be quite impactful on audiences. I often find that organizations can establish this same effect by making major changes that become accepted ways of life within the organizations.

It is not always easy to perform a decrescendo. Organizations that spend time thinking, planning, and institutionalizing change see high performance and employee satisfaction. Moving from loud to soft often requires a lot of resounding work, including town hall meetings, leadership reinforcement at ceremonies, institutionalizing new values through existing systems and performance-management systems, and rewarding new behaviors established by reinforcing new cultural values.

Rhythmic Reflection 9 - Target customers with positive surprises and develop members to increase satisfaction.

- What opportunities exist to create positive surprises for your customers in the future?

- What opportunities exist to create positive surprises for employees or other stakeholders?
- Have you analyzed your satisfaction surveys for opportunities to secure the right dynamics?

Orchestrating Leadership

Having leaders involved in the vision and strategy is critical to creating an upbeat rhythm. Leaders should reinforce the need for ongoing improvement and sustainability. All leaders must reward and reinforce the right behaviors associated with employee commitment, productivity, efficiency, and effectiveness. It also involves all organizational systems that reinforce the concept of ongoing evaluation and improvement as a way of life.

If adopting new behaviors to improve productivity, it certainly helps when leaders are involved in communicating and evaluating the implementation. Human resource initiatives—training, planning, implementation, and use of developmental plans—and other positive organizational initiatives were often completed because the line managers' evaluations were affected by their levels of commitment and accountability in these areas.

It certainly helps when you engage top leadership in all key systems that support the organization. If you want to retain winning talent, start succession planning efforts at the very top of the executive ranks. They should be key participants in the process. When they are involved, it is surprising how easily commitment follows throughout the leadership systems—and ultimately throughout the organization.

Rhythmic Reflection 10 - Elicit leadership in taking a key role in reinforcing behaviors that provide a competitive advantage.

What external communication plans have you developed to support the vision and strategy?

- Who are the key leaders and stakeholders you need to involve to achieve the required commitment?
- How can you engage leadership when communicating to generate excitement and motivation?

THE FINAL CURTAIN

AS WE NEAR THE END of this score, which is directed at improving your results, we certainly do not want to see the final curtain. To avoid the final curtain and ensure a lasting performance of greatness, I would like to share a few final musical points.

In order to optimize our abilities, I often think of those letters that some of us might remember as we struggled in our early attempts to learn the musical scale. Some of you might remember E-G-B-D-F (in a scale), which was an acronym for "every good boy does fine."

Every Good Business Demands Focus

In business, the acronym can be changed to "every great business demands focus." By intensifying your melody and following the steps to executing these efforts, a great melody is a natural result. You must not forget, however, that your final score includes a great melody that is pleasing to your audiences. This means having the right talent that hits the right notes and stays in tune to ensure that the sound becomes pleasing for the performance and for the long term. Constantly adjusting to changing needs and adapting to changing forces can ensure longevity.

Designing the harmony that accompanies that melody is critical. Customers and employees need to believe that everyone is pulling in the same direction. They both can perceive when the left hand does not know what the right hand is doing and vice versa. This requires an organization system that is in balance with leaders who ensure that their teams are orchestrated to provide that blend and support the unique sound and rhapsody of sustainability.

To really score big, however, an organization requires rhythm. It is often the final ingredient to a great piece of music. Accelerating to an upbeat tempo can only happen when there is constant evaluation and integration of improvement. The organization needs to establish an ensemble that looks at how the organization is renewing itself and ensuring that everyone is singing from the same sheet of music to maintain that distinct melody, the sound chords associated with harmony, and the beat of continuous improvement. A constant support system and leadership involvement creates excitement, a culture of feedback, and optimization for ongoing success.

The beat goes on!

As we review our final score, remember to keep these thoughts in mind:

- *Intensify* the melody.
- *Design* the harmony.
- *Accelerate* the rhythm.

THE FINAL SCORE

Intensify the Melody

- *Incorporate* innovative changes that include proactively scanning and benchmarking best practices.
- *Nourish* customer satisfaction by looking for ways to surprise your customers with unique products, services, and other customer-focused actions.
- *Take* time to satisfy stakeholders in unique ways by assuming social responsibility and providing opportunities for balance in your workforce.
- *Ensure* that values are aligned to create positive customer expectations.
- *Never* take your eyes off the sheet of music. Keep alert to the environment and conduct periodic surveys for assessment and adjustment.
- *Stay* in touch with your audiences to increase your understanding.
- *Integrate* opportunities to reinforce the right values in your organization and maximize the process by eliminating functional silos.
- *Focus* on retaining winning talent, particularly during times of change.
- *Yield* to customer and competitive data for the right clues and timing of your goals and objectives.

Design the Harmony

- *Design* the organization so that it can sustain itself.
- *Ensure* that you reinforce the strategy and institutionalize key values and components (processes/roles) that support the strategy.
- *Seek* the continuous-improvement beat that helps sustain organizational effectiveness and efficiency by measuring.
- *Integrate* all elements of the support system.
- *Gain* alignment by paying attention to values and principles and supporting important behaviors and attitudes.
- *Navigate* so that you organize around processes. Ensure that team and customer values serve as a foundation for hiring, reinforcement, and reward systems.

Accelerate the Rhythm

- *Add* large-scale organizational redesign efforts to maximize results.
- *Combine* leadership reinforcement and team collaboration to quicken the tempo, but take the time to reflect on learning to sustain success.
- *Continue* to look at all internal components and external forces that affect the organization to stay in tune and redesign for greatness.
- *Engage* people in strategy advancement, technological changes, and innovation. Maintain a tremolo of satisfaction with engagement.
- *Look* for ways to provide time and reinforce creativity and innovation.
- *Ensure* that leaders are a key part of the communication plan—and include organization systems that support improvement.

- *Reinforce* positive values that focus on retaining winning talent.
- *Accept* feedback and proactively collect information that will allow the organization to sing from the same sheet of music.
- *Target* customers with positive surprises and develop members to increase satisfaction.
- *Elicit* leadership in taking a key role in reinforcing behaviors that provide a competitive advantage.

www.ingramcontent.com/pod-product-compliance
Lightning Source LLC
Chambersburg PA
CBHW021026180526
45163CB00005B/2140